The Enigma of Faith

A Believer's Handbook

Dr. Kevin Abankwa

The Enigma of Faith

ISBN: 979-8-9879189-8-2

Scripture References

The Enigma of Faith

CONTENTS

DEDICATION & ACKNOWLEDGMENTS

Thanks be to God whom I acknowledge in all my ways, and has directed and guided me to complete this book.

To my beautiful and supportive wife (Awo) and my wonderful children (Kenji, Kayden, and Kaila) all of you have been my inspiration to share my gifts to the world.

CHAPTER 1
Teaching Christ

Jesus Christ is the charter of humankind. The Scripture is emphatic on the Word being with the Father before the foundations of the earth.

> In the beginning was the Word, and the Word was with God, and the Word was God. ² He was in the beginning with God. ³ All things were made through Him, and without Him nothing was made that was made. ⁴ In Him was life, and the life was the light of men. ⁵ And the light shines in the darkness, and the darkness did not comprehend it.
> John 1:1-5

From Genesis to Revelation, we can study and understand that Jesus Christ is revealed to us in a different light to many generations throughout scriptures. No wonder when Apostle Paul was writing to the believers at Ephesus about the newness of life that they have, he made it a point to highlight the subject called Christ. He said in Ephesians 4:20-21

> But you have not so **learned Christ**, ²¹ if indeed you have heard Him and have been taught by Him, as the truth is in Jesus

Christ is <u>the</u> subject within the schooling system of the Life that He has given to every believer. This is what I have termed as **The Quinquepartite Mystery of Christ.**

<u>The Quinquepartite Mystery of Christ.</u>
I would like to take you through what one of the prophets of old said concerning Christ:

For unto us a Child is born, Unto us a Son is given;
And the government will be upon His shoulder.
And His **name** will be called Wonderful, Counselor,
Mighty God, Everlasting Father, Prince of Peace.
Isaiah 9:6

In the book of Isaiah, the Holy Spirit gives us a picture of the Savior. The Hebrew word *Shêm*, translated in the scripture above as *name*, also translates to the word *character*. Now, let's go back to Isaiah 9:6 and replace the word *name* with *character*.

For unto us a Child is born, Unto us a Son is given;
And the government will be upon His shoulder.
And His *character* will be called Wonderful, Counselor,
Mighty God, Everlasting Father, Prince of Peace.
Isaiah 9:6

The character description of Christ is given as Wonderful, Counselor, Mighty God, Everlasting Father, and Prince of Peace. In a few verses prior, we notice how the Savior will be known.

Therefore the Lord Himself will give you a sign: Behold,
the virgin shall conceive and bear a Son, and shall call His
name Immanuel.
Isaiah 7:14

Here, we see another description of Christ. He is Immanuel, which is translated as *God with us*. For God to be with us in the flesh, He had to come through the womb of a woman. When we read the synoptic Gospels, we see the storyline of how this occurred. Let us look at the Gospel according to Matthew.

But while he thought about these things, behold, an
angel of the Lord appeared to him in a dream, saying,
"Joseph, son of David, do not be afraid to take to you

Mary your wife, for that which is conceived in her is of the Holy Spirit. ²¹ And she will bring forth a Son, and you shall call His name Jesus, for He will save His people from their sins."
Matthew 1:20-21

In the scripture above, the angel introduced the name Jesus and immediately gave a reason for the name: "...*for He will save His people from their sins.*" Thus, He is *Yeshua*, the name announced by the angel in Hebrew, which translates to the savior, rescuer, or deliverer.

Jesus, the name that the Western world has come to know, is God Almighty as the son of man. Jesus Christ, or Jesus the Christ, is the Son of God. The Scripture says in the book of John:

And many other signs truly did Jesus in the presence of his disciples, which are not written in this book:
³¹ But these are written, that ye might believe that **Jesus is the Christ, the Son of God**; and that believing ye might have life through his name.
John 20:30-31

Christ or *Christos* means anointed, which is derived from the Greek word *chrio*, meaning to anoint or consecrate to an office. After Jesus was baptized and tempted by the devil, He went to Nazareth (*see* Luke 3:21-22; 4:1-15). He had begun His ministry during this time, and His fame spread through the neighboring regions. Scripture indicates that Jesus then went to the synagogue on the Sabbath day.

And He was handed the book of the prophet Isaiah. And when He had opened the book, He found the place where it was written:
¹⁸ "The Spirit of the Lord is upon Me, Because He has anointed Me
To preach the gospel to the poor;

He has sent Me to heal the brokenhearted,
To proclaim liberty to the captives
And recovery of sight to the blind,
To set at liberty those who are oppressed;
[19] To proclaim the acceptable year of the Lord."
[20] Then He closed the book, and gave it back to the
attendant and sat down. And the eyes of all who were in
the synagogue were fixed on Him.
Luke 4:17-20

Your life's ultimate purpose begins when you locate yourself in the Word of God, for everyone's identity or DNA is sourced from the Word of God because we are born of the Word.

Having been born again, not of corruptible seed
but incorruptible, through the word of God which lives
and abides forever.
1 Peter 1:23

1. The Person of Christ

The first of the quinquepartite elements is the person of Christ. Let us look at the following scripture:

In Him you also *trusted,* after you heard the word of
truth, the gospel of your salvation; in whom also, having
believed, you were sealed with the Holy Spirit of promise
Ephesians 1:13

For as the body is one and has many members, but all
the members of that one body, being many, are one
body, so also *is* Christ.
1 Corinthians 12:12

Christ in the person of Jesus manifested Himself to the World. This was done by becoming the son of man.

> Philip found Nathanael and said to him, "We have
> found Him of whom Moses in the law, and also the
> prophets, wrote—Jesus of Nazareth, the son of Joseph."
> John 1:45

The human nature that Jesus carried is exhibited throughout Scripture. He was hungry, angry, tired, and slept just like any man would (*see* Mark 11:12, Matthew 21:12-13, Mark 3:5, John 4:6, Mark 4:38-40).

2. The Place Called Christ.

From the Scriptures, we know that there is a place called Christ, which is a spiritual location. In addressing where we belong as believers and where we're located spiritually, scripture tells us that we're in a spiritual or heavenly abode in Christ.

> And raised *us* up together, and made *us* sit together in
> the heavenly *places* in Christ Jesus.
> Ephesians 2:6

When you're in the place called Christ, the enemy is made your footstool, and you are in a position of dominion and power. This is a place where every believer has to abide–that is–to reside and remain. The place that we have in Christ is an actual environment with rules that govern that location. Referring to the new life believers are given, the Word of God says:

> For you died, and your life is hidden with Christ in
> God.
> Colossians 3:3

That is the most secure location anyone can be. The moment we become born again, we are transported into Christ because we now share His eternal life. This life that we have hidden in Christ is also in God. Glory to God!

Now, this is a spiritual place. This is the place that governs believers' affairs as they walk with the Lord. It is critical for every believer to be cognizant and conscious of this fact. The more an individual is aware of their state of being in Christ, the more they are in tune with the Holy Spirit. Thus, we abide in Him, and He in us (*see* John 6:56). Christ is our place of dwelling, and everything we do is done with that in mind.

For in Him we live and move and have our being, as also some of your own poets have said, 'For we are also His offspring.'
Acts 17:28

3. Christ is a Law

As we have just learned about the place called Christ, it is the law of Christ that governs. The environment of any place is governed or dictated by the law(s) that govern that environment. On Earth, it is the laws on and around this planet that create our environment.

Let's be more specific and use the Moon as an example. The laws that operate in space prevent us from undertaking certain activities over there. Unless we study, understand, and rightly apply those laws, we cannot get the results that we desire. So, what is the law of Christ?

Bear one another's burdens, and so fulfill the law of Christ.
Galatians 6:2

The scripture above tells us about what action to take to satisfy the law. Let's take some more scriptures.

For the law of the Spirit of life in Christ Jesus has made me free from the law of sin and death.
Romans 8:2

It takes a law to veto another law. The law in Christ makes

us free from the bondage of sin and death. When Christ fulfilled the law given to the children of Israel, He brought the law to perfection. Let us hear the words of Jesus.

> Do not think that I came to destroy the Law or the Prophets. I did not come to destroy but to fulfill.
> Matthew 5:17

The law that operates in the life of a believer should not be seen as a stringent set of rules a believer has to follow to gain salvation or eternal life. No, the law of Christ is simple. The Apostle Paul puts it this way:

> For all the law is fulfilled in one word, *even* in this: "You shall love your neighbor as yourself."
> Galatians 5:14

Walking in love is functioning in love. We know that God is Love. He is the embodiment, fabric, and constituent of love (*see* 1 John 4:8). An orange tree produces oranges. If an orange tree produces apples, that tree will be in question because it defies its natural order. In the same way, we who are born from Him should exhibit the nature and character of the Father. God demonstrated His love by sending His first begotten Son unto us so that we can receive salvation.

4. Christ is a School

Any form of educational system or structure set to impact knowledge and instructions under the tutorship of teachers can be described as a school. In the Kingdom of God, He has set facilities in place to help the growth of a believer.

> And He Himself gave some *to be* apostles, some prophets, some evangelists, and some pastors and teachers, 12 for the equipping of the saints for the work of ministry, for the edifying of the body of Christ, 13 till we all

> come to the unity of the faith and of the knowledge of
> the Son of God, to a perfect man, to the measure of the
> stature of the fullness of Christ;
> Ephesians 4:11-13

The goal is for believers to grow and not to remain as "babes" (*see* Ephesians 4:14-16). That means there are certain subjects we are supposed to study, understand, and apply to grow in Christ as children of God. We see these subjects listed in Hebrews 6.

> Therefore, leaving the discussion of the
> elementary *principles* of Christ, let us go on to [a]perfection,
> not laying again the foundation of repentance from dead
> works and of faith toward God, 2 of the doctrine of
> baptisms, of laying on of hands, of resurrection of the
> dead, and of eternal judgment. 3 And this we will do if
> God permits.
>
> 4 For *it is* impossible for those who were once
> enlightened, and have tasted the heavenly gift, and have
> become partakers of the Holy Spirit, 5 and have tasted the
> good word of God and the powers of the age to
> come, 6 if they fall away, to renew them again to
> repentance, since they crucify again for themselves the
> Son of God, and put *Him* to an open shame.
> Hebrews 6:1-6

The utterances of God are the instructional learnings a believer goes through to be fully matured. You can consider it a body of knowledge prepared for every believer. The Holy Spirit directs every child of God through these learnings. Every believer needs to go through the "first principles."

> For though by this time you ought to be teachers, you

need someone to teach you again the <u>first principles</u> of the oracles of God; and you have come to need milk and not solid food.
Hebrews 5:12

These first principles are the foundational or fundamental understanding of Christ a believer must build upon that foundation. Let us go through Hebrews 6:1-6 and list these essential subjects.

As the Spirit of God leads a believer through these topics, the duration that one spends on a topic is set by the Spirit of God. I am going through these schooling systems myself, and the Lord teaches me new things all the time, even on topics I've previously studied in detail. That is how the Lord operates. Even when you think you have covered all the topics that need to be covered on a subject, He shows you that His ways are indeed past finding out.

As a believer ascends toward the knowledge of God, the believer is supposed to become more and more skillful in the word of righteousness. What is the word of righteousness? Is it the same as just saying the Word of God?

For everyone who partakes only of milk is unskilled in the <u>word of righteousness</u>, for he is a babe. ¹⁴*But solid food belongs to those who are of full age, that is, those who by reason of use have their <u>senses exercised to discern both good and evil</u>.*
Hebrews 5:13-14

We see here that the growth of a believer is intentional. It is planned, and it requires excising and using the faculties that connect us to our God, who is spirit, for we worship Him in spirit and in truth. The word of righteousness can be broken down into the following:

- The way of righteousness
- The righteousness of God
- Christ Jesus, our righteousness
- God's righteousness
- The Lord, our righteousness
- Righteousness of faith
- The righteousness of saints.

Righteousness doesn't equal good works, and unrighteousness doesn't equal evil works. The easiest revelation concerning righteousness is in Genesis 2:9.

*And out of the ground made the Lord God to grow every tree that is pleasant to the sight, and good for food; **the tree of life** also in the midst of the garden, and the **tree of knowledge of good and evil.***

Only the tree of life produces life. Thus, the instruction of righteousness bears the fruits of life. Good and evil are from the same tree, and its harvest is death. Hence, good works can be done but might yield death.

The scope of this book will not permit me to go through each of these. However, let us list the various topics given in Hebrews 6 for believers to study. These topics were intentionally listed in order so believers can literally start a journey of perpetual growth by tackling each subject.

1. Elementary principles of Christ (*See* Acts 20:20-22)
2. Doctrine of baptisms
3. Laying on of hands
4. Resurrection of the dead
5. Eternal judgment
6. Tasting heavenly gifts
7. Partakers of the Holy Spirit
8. Tasting the good Word of God

9. Tasting of the powers of the age to come

Imagine a believer laying hands on an individual without first understanding repentance and faith towards God, which is part of the elementary principles of Christ. Now imagine what more that same believer can do with a full knowledge and understanding of the subject. The second most important thing for every person after salvation is the knowledge of Christ, for He is the way, the truth, and the life.

> Who desires all men to be saved and to come to the knowledge of the truth.
> 1 Timothy 2:4

I pray the Lord will grant me the ability and grace to write on each of those topics as listed in Hebrews 6. I have been raised as a Christian all my life, and I continue to learn new things on each of those topics on a regular basis.

The last part of the quinquepartite mystery of Christ is:

5. Christ: Our Garment

For us to understand what we mean by Christ being our garment, we would have to go back to the time of the ceremonial garment worn during times of service not long after the priesthood was introduced.

> And you shall make for them linen trousers to cover their nakedness; they shall reach from the waist to the thighs. 43They shall be on Aaron and on his sons when they come into the tabernacle of meeting, or when they come near the altar to minister in the holy place, that they do not incur iniquity and die. It shall be a statute forever to him and his descendants after him.
> Exodus 24:42-43

The instructions were given to Aaron and his sons to have

that covering so they didn't incur iniquity and die. The garment provided them with a form of protection when they entered the holy place. When we see Christ as our garment, we give no part of our body to be exposed for the enemy to use.

But put on the Lord Jesus Christ, and make no provision for the flesh, to fulfill its lusts.
Romans 13:14

The Lord Jesus Christ is our garment that covers every part of our body, from the crown of our heads to the soles of our feet. He is our covering, for He has given us covered protection. Always maintain this consciousness, and you will forever be victorious against the lusts of the flesh. Again, we see in scripture the significance of putting on Christ in the epistle to the Galatians.

For as many of you as were baptized into Christ have put on Christ.
Galatians 3:27

When you were baptized, did you know that you were baptized into Christ and now have on Christ as a garment? How amazing! *Hallelujah!* No wonder we can go before God in boldness, knowing that when He sees us, He sees Christ!

From Genesis to Revelation, we see Christ as we read through the scripture. The scripture <u>does not</u> have eternal life; scripture <u>points to the giver of eternal life</u>. Hence, life is not in scripture; life is in the person of scripture, who is Jesus Christ. You can read the scripture, but if you don't go to whom the scripture points to, you cannot have eternal life.

You search the Scriptures, for in them you think you have eternal life; and these are they which testify of Me.
John 5:39

Now, let's look at a conversation between Cleopas and his companion on their way to Emmaus.

> And certain of those who were with us went to the tomb and found it just as the women had said; but Him they did not see." ²⁵Then He said to them, "O foolish ones, and slow of heart to believe in all that the prophets have spoken! ²⁶Ought not the Christ to have suffered these things and to enter into His glory?" ²⁷And beginning at Moses and all the Prophets, He expounded to them in all the Scriptures the things concerning Himself.
> Luke 24:24-27

The Lord Jesus expounded to these men on the scriptures and showed them that all scripture indeed points to Him. So, what is the sum of scripture? The answer is summed up beautifully in Paul's second letter to Timothy.

> And that from childhood you have known the Holy Scriptures, which are able to make you wise for salvation through faith which is in Christ Jesus.
> 2 Timothy 3:15

The purpose of scripture is to make one wise for salvation. **This is a principle**, meaning its application is beyond just being saved and becoming a believer. After you become a believer, if you are in a bad situation–it may be finances, sickness, marital issues, family issues, and other challenges–the scriptures can make you wise to receive salvation from that situation through faith, which is in Christ Jesus. Principles in God's Word are what I call "golden keys" because they open multiple doors in a believer's life when they are understood and applied correctly.

The apostles encountered the Living Word in the personality of Jesus Christ. It is the wisdom a believer has that makes them bold. This is because Christ has been made our wisdom (*see* 1 Corinthians 1:30). The apostles' wisdom demonstrated in the form of boldness was made known to many.

> Now when they saw the boldness of Peter and John, and perceived that they were uneducated and untrained men, they marveled. And they realized that they had been with Jesus.
>
> Acts 4:13

Christ, being our garment, gives us access and passage to the Father.

> Jesus said to him, "I am the way, the truth, and the life. No one comes to the Father except through Me.
>
> John 14:6

Under the old covenant, access to the Most Holy Place was done only by the high priest. The passageway was covered with what we can describe as a garment/curtain/veil. Now, when Jesus was on the cross before His body was broken and released His Spirit, the Word of God says the garment in the temple was torn.

> The sun was darkened, and the veil of the temple was torn in two.
>
> Luke 23:45

We no longer need a garment of separation. *Hallelujah!* Christ has become our garment, a garment that is never removed. Wherever we go, we carry His presence with us. Every place we go, Christ goes. As you step out today, have this in mind: *You are covered by Him.* The same "garment" called Christ protects you from the stratagems of the enemy. Brothers and sisters in Christ, you are covered on every side! Praise be to His name forevermore.

CHAPTER 2
Allegorical & Similitude Significance

Scripture is filled with allegories and similitudes. The purpose of this book and chapter is not to be academic but to portray a balance of spiritual realities and physical experiences. Can allegories and similitudes describe spiritual realities? Do they have any significance in the gospel?

Balance is critical when it comes to our walk with the Lord. Balancing spiritual realities and physical experiences positions us on a path that enables us to better understand the ways of God. Allegories and similitudes cannot perfectly explain spiritual truths because they are in different realms. However, they do have significance because they act as a "shadow," so we have an idea or understanding of a place we might not have access to at another point in time.

Understanding the spiritual realities existing in our daily walk is a prerequisite for living a triumphant life in Christ. Spiritual realities are active for believers as well as unbelievers, the same way the sun shines on believers as well as unbelievers. Just as the physical world, the spiritual world is regulated by laws. The Word of God is the underpinning upholding the universe and all its operations.

In reference to Jesus Christ, the scripture indicates that He often spoke in parables to the people. Parables are short allegories.

Jesus spoke all these things to the crowd in parables; he did not say anything to them without using a parable. 35 So was fulfilled what was spoken through the prophet: "I will open my mouth in parables, I will utter things hidden since the creation of the world."
Matthew 13:34-35

An introduction into the hidden things is sometimes done

in the way of allegories and similitudes. Faith is a spiritual phenomenon; therefore, we will need a vehicle (allegories and similitudes) to carry us into reality so that when we are settled in our understanding, we will no longer need them.

One day, Jesus spoke to a multitude that had gathered to hear from Him, and He talked about a sower who went out to sow.

> On the same day Jesus went out of the house and sat by the sea. ² And great multitudes were gathered together to Him, so that He got into a boat and sat; and the whole multitude stood on the shore.
> ³ Then He spoke many things to them in parables, saying: "Behold, a sower went out to sow. ⁴ And as he sowed, some seed fell by the wayside; and the birds came and devoured them. ⁵ Some fell on stony places, where they did not have much earth; and they immediately sprang up because they had no depth of earth. ⁶ But when the sun was up they were scorched, and because they had no root they withered away. ⁷ And some fell among thorns, and the thorns sprang up and choked them. ⁸ But others fell on good ground and yielded a crop: some a hundredfold, some sixty, some thirty. ⁹ He who has ears to hear, let him hear!"
> Matthew 13:1-9

The Lord ended this parable by indicating in verse nine, "he who has ears to hear, let him hear." Jesus was communicating a spiritual reality requiring an ear opened to spiritual realities to comprehend. I can imagine His disciples discussing among themselves what the parable conveyed until they finally approached the Lord and enquired the meaning of it. In answering the disciples, He made it known to them that the parable was to conceal a mystery.

> He answered and said to them, "Because it has been given to you to know the mysteries of the kingdom of

<u>heaven</u>, but to them it has not been given.
Matthew 13:11

The kingdom of heaven is a spiritual place, and the functions and dealings in that place are mysteries. However, these mysteries have been given to us to know. *Praise the Lord!*

This means we have access to the knowledge of spiritual realities; it does not necessarily mean we *know* them. Therefore, the apostles accessed and enquired from the Living Word the hidden truth in the parable. Jesus revealed to the apostles the spiritual truth of the parable:

"Therefore hear the parable of the sower: [19] When anyone hears the word of the kingdom, and does not understand it, then the wicked one comes and snatches away what was sown in his heart. This is he who received seed by the wayside. [20] But he who received the seed on stony places, this is he who hears the word and immediately receives it with joy; [21] yet he has no root in himself, but endures only for a while. For when tribulation or persecution arises because of the word, immediately he stumbles. [22] Now he who received seed among the thorns is he who hears the word, and the cares of this world and the deceitfulness of riches choke the word, and he becomes unfruitful. [23] But he who received seed on the good ground is he who hears the word and understands it, who indeed bears fruit and produces: some a hundredfold, some sixty, some thirty."
Matthew 13:18-23

Wow, this is amazing. Here, we see spiritual activities taking place in the lives of individuals in the spiritual realm, and we see the effects in the physical environment. The Lord used a parable to convey a similitude of the physical and spiritual realities in order to introduce a hidden truth.

Still within chapter 13 of Matthew, the Lord Jesus spoke of another parable that I want to bring to your attention: the parable of the wheat and the tares. The Lord wanted to convey another truth to His audience. This time, it was about the Kingdom of God.

> Another parable He put forth to them, saying: "The kingdom of heaven is like a man who sowed good seed in his field; 25 but while men slept, his enemy came and sowed tares among the wheat and went his way. 26 But when the grain had sprouted and produced a crop, then the tares also appeared. 27 So the servants of the owner came and said to him, 'Sir, did you not sow good seed in your field? How then does it have tares?' 28 He said to them, 'An enemy has done this.' The servants said to him, 'Do you want us then to go and gather them up?' 29 But he said, 'No, lest while you gather up the tares you also uproot the wheat with them. 30 Let both grow together until the harvest, and at the time of harvest I will say to the reapers, "First gather together the tares and bind them in bundles to burn them, but gather the wheat into my barn."
> Matthew 13:24-30

As you read through the scriptures, it's important not to forget the cultural setting. Therefore, having a Hebraic perspective can shed more light on your understanding rather than reading and studying the scriptures with the mindset of your cultural understanding.

Jesus was speaking to people who were primarily farmers. The Lord used the activity of farming to talk about the Kingdom of God. Again, since He spoke mysteries that were only given to the disciples to know the spiritual implications, He later explained what spiritual truth the parable conveyed. Jesus did not volunteer to reveal the truth hidden in the parables; the disciples inquired to know. When we enquire of the Lord the things that have been given to us to know, He always answers.

After the disciples enquired about the meaning of the

parable, Jesus explained the parables of the tares of the field to them.

> He answered and said to them: "He who sows the good seed is the Son of Man. **38** The field is the world, the good seeds are the sons of the kingdom, but the tares are the sons of the wicked one. **39** The enemy who sowed them is the devil, the harvest is the end of the age, and the reapers are the angels. **40** Therefore as the tares are gathered and burned in the fire, so it will be at the end of this age. **41** The Son of Man will send out His angels, and they will gather out of His kingdom all things that offend, and those who practice lawlessness, **42** and will cast them into the furnace of fire. There will be wailing and gnashing of teeth. **43** Then the righteous will shine forth as the sun in the kingdom of their Father. He who has ears to hear, let him hear!
> Matthew 13:37-43

I would like to spend some time on this parable because it is crucial to our discussion on spiritual realities. The last statement of verse 43 indicates that we're dealing with spiritual matters, and we need spiritual understanding to fathom their implications.

In the interpretation of the parable, the Lord Jesus indicates that *"the field is the world..."* This parable is *not* about the church but about two kingdoms (God and devil) and their interaction with the world. We are given a clear picture of how the sons of the kingdom and of the devil will end up. The devil is a creature himself, as he was created. The devil cannot create a human; however, any human who doesn't accept Christ and thus lives in an environment away from Christ is a child of the wicked one.

Everyone was birthed out of a seed. There is a corruptible seed that every person is birthed from when they come into this world. There is an incorruptible seed that a believer is birthed from when they're born again (*see* 1 Peter 1:23). The incorruptible seed is the Word of God as we read in Matthew 13:1-9. That is why when a believer accepts Christ, they become a new creature–a peculiar type of being.

So, since the Word of God is a seed, it matters how and where it is planted and nurtured to bring forth all the fruits that the Word is capable of producing. A believing heart is the manure needed for the incorruptible seed (Word of God) to bear fruit. Right from the day a believer accepts Christ. It starts with them believing in their heart that Jesus is Lord. This is a principle of salvation; hence, all the other fruits that come from salvation are also fulfilled in the same manner.

If you understand this, then you will not be surprised when you read the portion of scripture that says that Jesus wasn't able to do any mighty work in Nazareth because the people had an unbelieving heart (*see* Matthew 13:53-58).

Let us take another example from the teaching of the Master. As Jesus started His ministry of reconciliation when He was on Earth, He continued to use the environment or manner of living of the people to convey truths to them. In John 10, He introduces Himself as a good shepherd.

> "Most assuredly, I say to you, he who does not enter the sheepfold by the door, but climbs up some other way, the same is a thief and a robber. 2 But he who enters by the door is the shepherd of the sheep. 3 To him the doorkeeper opens, and the sheep hear his voice; and he calls his own sheep by name and leads them out. 4 And when he brings out his own sheep, he goes before them; and the sheep follow him, for they know his voice. 5 Yet they will by no means follow a stranger, but will flee from him, for they do not know the voice of strangers." 6 Jesus used this illustration, but they did not understand the things which He spoke to them.
> John 10:1-6

As primarily farmers and fishermen, they understood what

it takes to protect sheep. What they didn't understand was that Jesus was talking about Himself for the people to understand His role as a good shepherd, a caretaker, and a protector. He had to use a scenario or phenomenon that they fully understood in order to introduce a spiritual truth. Jesus as well as His apostles employed this technique in talking about the truth of God's Word, and this is evident throughout scripture.

> Then Jesus said to them again, "Most assuredly, I say to you, I am the door of the sheep. 8 All
> who ever came before Me are thieves and robbers, but the sheep did not hear them. 9 I am the door. If anyone enters by Me, he will be saved, and will go in and out and find pasture. 10 The thief does not come except to steal, and to kill, and to destroy. I have come that they may have life, and that they may have it more abundantly. 11 "I am the good shepherd. The good shepherd gives His life for the sheep.
> John 10:7-11

In the next section I will introduce the main subject for this book which is: Faith. Before we get into that subject it's important that I spend some time illustrating the importance of allegories and their use in explaining spiritual truths.

Every individual, Christian or non-Christian, interacts with a parallel realm (physical & spiritual) daily. Just as the physical world has laws, the spiritual world also has laws. As good people, out of the goodness of their hearts, use the physical/natural laws to invent things to the benefit of mankind, evil people, out of the evil treasures of their hearts, use the same physical laws to invent things that are detrimental to humanity. Therefore, spiritual laws are open to everyone, just as physical laws. As believers, we cannot be ignorant of this pertinent truth. If we are ignorant of this, it will affect everything about us, including our worship to God (*see* John 4:24).

CHAPTER 3
Faith

"Your conviction determines your faith; your faith determines your actions; and your actions determines your possessions."
Dr. Abankwa

Faith is perhaps one of the most critical phenomena of the Christian faith. At the foundational level, a believer must know that they have faith, because without faith they could not have been saved.

For by grace you have been saved through faith, and that not of yourselves; it is the gift of God, [9] not of works, lest anyone should boast.
Ephesians 2:8-9

If you are a believer reading this, I would like you to know that you do have faith. One might ask, *"How did I receive faith?"* When you received Christ, God also imparted a level of faith into your spirit.

For I say, through the grace given to me, to everyone who is among you, not to think of himself more highly than he ought to think, but to think soberly, as God has dealt to each one a <u>measure of faith</u>. .
Romans 12:3

Now that we understand we do have a measure of faith, let's take some time to understand what faith is according to God's Word.

Now faith is the substance of things hoped for, the evidence of things not seen.
Hebrews 11:1

I would like us to go through different translations of Hebrews 11:1

Now faith is the assurance (the confirmation, the title deed) of the things [we] hope for, being the proof of things [we] do not see and the conviction of their reality [faith perceiving as real fact what is not revealed to the senses].
(AMPC)

Now faith is the assurance of things hoped for, the conviction of things not seen.
(RSV)

And faith is of things hoped for a confidence, of matters not seen a conviction.
(YLT)

Faith is a spiritual element with the ability to produce physical fulfillment. In other words, faith brings the unseen into the physical. This means faith is eternal.

For our light affliction, which is but for a moment, is working for us a far more exceeding and eternal weight of glory, [18] while we do not look at the things which are seen, but at the things which are not seen. For the things which are seen are temporary, but the things which are not seen are eternal.
2 Corinthians 4:17-18

Thus, by faith, we have access to the spiritual realm to make reality: the physical, tangible things that are needed. Reading further, the third verse of Hebrews 11 states:

By faith we understand that the worlds were framed by the word of God, so that the things which are seen were not made of things which are visible.

From the scriptures above we understand that faith is a substance that is not of matter. Can a spiritual element be of substance but not of matter? Absolutely!

An example is when spiritual bodies manifest themselves in the physical.

> All flesh is not the same flesh, but there
> is one kind of flesh of men, another flesh of animals,
> another of fish, and another of birds.
> 40 There are also celestial bodies and terrestrial bodies;
> but the glory of the celestial is one, and the glory of the
> terrestrial is another. 41 There is one glory of the sun,
> another glory of the moon, and another glory of the stars;
> for one star differs from another star in glory.
> 1 Corinthians 14:39-41

When Jesus resurrected, He had a different body: a glorified body. This body was of substance because His disciples were able to hold him. However, it was not of matter because Jesus could appear and disappear whenever he pleased.

> 36 Now as they said these things, Jesus Himself stood in
> the midst of them, and said to them, "Peace to
> you." 37 But they were terrified and frightened, and
> supposed they had seen a spirit....
> 39 Behold My hands and My feet, that it is I
> Myself. Handle Me and see, for a spirit does not have flesh
> and bones as you see I have."
> Luke 24:36-37, 39

Now we understand that the resurrected, glorious body of Jesus was of substance but not of matter. The classical definition of matter is any substance that has mass and takes up space by virtue of its volume. As a scientist and an engineer, I know that matter such as a body is *not* supposed to have the ability to go through walls.

For instance, before a house is built, all the material that is needed is identified and purchased. The material is the substance of the house hoped for, the evidence of the house not yet built or seen. The house started with an imagination (hope), and that hope was translated into faith (material for construction).

Yet Jesus appeared to His disciples in a substantial body and to His body after the resurrection without matter, which enabled Him to appear and disappear. He is the author and finisher of our faith, and we look up to Him as the embodiment of all the faith we can ever have (*see* Hebrews 12:2). Therefore, our faith is of substance and not of matter. We also know that the Word became flesh (substance and matter) and dwelt among us (*see* John 1:14), and after He resurrected, He was still of flesh (substance without matter). Faith then comes from the Word of God that we hear.

So then faith comes by hearing, and hearing by the word of God.
Romans 10:17

We hear His Word by reading and listening. It is within that same realm of faith that God created the universe and its operations. This faith that we are discussing is the faith given to every believer, which is different from the unique gift of faith the Holy Spirit gives to certain believers as He wills.

But the manifestation of the Spirit is given to each one for the profit of all: **8** *for to one is given the word of wisdom through the Spirit, to another the word of knowledge through the same Spirit,* **9** *to another faith by the same Spirit, to another gifts of healings by the same Spirit.*
1 Corinthians 12:7-9

The discussion of the special gift of faith is beyond the

scope of this book, and I would not be able to discuss it thoroughly. However, I would like you to know that there is a difference between a believer's faith and the special gift of faith. Every gift God gives us comes in the form of a seed that needs to be nurtured in order to grow and bear fruit to profit everyone.

In an act of faith, Abel brought an acceptable sacrifice to God.

> By faith Abel offered to God a more excellent sacrifice
> than Cain, through which he obtained witness that he
> was righteous, God testifying of his gifts; and through it
> he being dead still speaks.
> Hebrews 11:4

Faith is an intangible force that can work with a substance (with or without matter), bringing the invisible into the physical realm (matter).

The most straightforward explanation I can use is money. Everybody knows the importance of money in terms of achieving physical things, whether real-estate properties or other possessions. In this physical world, money is the substance of things hoped for, the evidence of things not seen. Faith is like money physically.

In God's Kingdom, faith is what is needed to live and function. In this physical world, money is required to live and function. Both faith and money are substances with power. Faith is a utility that can only be used, and so is money. Faith is a substance without matter, while money is a substance with matter. Jesus said that one cannot serve two masters.

> "No one can serve two masters; for either he will hate
> the one and love the other, or else he will be loyal to the
> one and despise the other. You cannot serve God
> and mammon."
> Matthew 6:24

This is a profound statement. In stating who the two masters are, Jesus mentions God and *mammon* (riches). This is because both are forces of a realm. The root of anything is the foundation or the vital force that holds that entity. The root of faith is God, and the love of money the root of all kinds of evil. This means some evil that exists will have its root traced to the love of money. That doesn't mean that money is evil; it is not.

We now know that every believer has a measure of faith. Without faith, it is impossible to please God and live the Christian life.

For example, let's say I want to acquire a company. It costs $1 million for the acquisition. I do not have the company yet, but when I pray to the Father, I have the mental image of the company acquisition. After I pray, I thank the Lord, and I decide to sow a seed (money) somewhere. The place where a seed is sown is crucial. This is one of the innumerable reasons why the ministry of the Holy Spirit is essential in the life of a believer.

> Take heed to yourself that you do not offer your burnt offerings in every place that you see; [14] but in the place which the Lord chooses, in one of your tribes, there you shall offer your burnt offerings, and there you shall do all that I command you.
> Deuteronomy 12:13-14

In the scripture above, God ensured that the Israelites only gave their burnt offerings in a specific place directed by Him. It is an error for a believer to think they can sow a seed at any church they want and it will be fine. God's universal church is comprised of many grounds of fertility. In the same way you wouldn't plant an orange seed anywhere, if you want to harvest oranges. Your seed for your harvest must be directed by the Lord. It might be to a person, a pastor, a church, or it might not even be in a church!

For our example, let's say I decided to sow a seed of $1,000 in a church. As I give the money in a church service, I pray and

I say:

> *"Father, as I sow this seed of $1,000, I call forth my harvest of the acquisition of the company. All the resources that I need are coming to me, and I believe in my heart; therefore, I confess with my mouth that I will get it. In Jesus name."*

As simple as this prayer is, it is prayed with understanding; therefore, it is effectual. A farmer plants with a purpose; no farmer sows a seed without any expectation of a harvest. Here, I'm talking about seed giving, which is only a part of the different types of giving according to God's Word. A seed is different from an offering, tithe, first fruit, etc.

What can happen after praying with an understanding of our actions? Sowing a seed, recognizing that a harvest is expected, and a faith-filled conviction in our hearts. Well, the Lord brings resources our way.

Continuing with our imaginary example. Now, somebody comes later and tells me about a program where I can apply to get funding for the purchase of the company. So, I diligently navigate the process and get the funding. The budget I receive is the substance of the company hoped for; this is evidence of the company not yet in my possession. I go through the acquisition process, and I exchange the finances for the company, and I've got my company! That's how faith works. You must always have faith for the next thing. You cannot apply yesterday's faith to today's actions.

Therefore, faith can be seen as an exchange rate in the spiritual realm, meaning you must have faith every day.

> For in it the righteousness of God is revealed from faith to faith; as it is written, "The just shall live by faith."
> Romans 1:17

In the Apostle Paul's letter to the believers in Rome, he quotes the prophet Habakkuk:

*"Behold the proud, His soul is not upright in him;
But <u>the just shall live by his faith</u>."*

Habakkuk 2:4

We are to live by faith every day. Faith becomes a legal tender in the spiritual realm, and it's always in operation. The faith needed to give an offering is different from the faith needed to offer the tithe, firstfruit, or seed for something required. All these types of giving require faith.

If this is understood, then you will understand when I make this statement: Christians can expand their income by using faith. Money in the hands of a believer can be a seed to bring harvest. Money in the hands of a believer is the substance for determining income that has no limits. As believers, whenever we work and receive money, there is one scripture that should always come to mind.

*Then you say in your heart, 'My power and the might of my hand have gained me this wealth.' [18] "And you shall remember the Lord your God, for it is **He who gives you power to get wealth**, that He may establish His covenant which He swore to your fathers, as it is this day.*
Deuteronomy 8:17-18

Wealth is attained with power. Power is the ability to do something, and for this discussion, it is the ability to make wealth. Having the power from the Lord alone does not make you wealthy. That power is an ability and has to be exercised to realize wealth. Hence, the power is a seed. Sometimes, the power is in the form of knowledge.

Anything the Father gives us is in a seed form.

This means faith, spiritual gifts, etc., come to us in a seed that must be planted and cultivated. Now that we understand faith, we have the "currency" to make certain transactions in the spirit, for we know that we are all spiritual beings, and the Father expects us to even worship Him in spirit and in truth.

In the next chapter, I will talk about walking in the Spirit. Before we can worship, praise, or do any spiritual activity, one must be able to walk in the Spirit.

CHAPTER 4
Walking in the Spirit

Walking is an act of consciousness. Walking also represents activities being undertaken. This is how the psalmist puts it:

Blessed is the man who <u>walks</u> not in the counsel of the ungodly, nor stands in the path of sinners, nor sits in the seat of the scornful; 2 But his delight is in the law of the Lord, and in His law he meditates day and night.
Psalms 1:1-2

So, what do I mean when I talk about walking in the Spirit?

To walk in the Spirit is to be in a continuous state of consciousness with the Lord—sensitive to His promptings—and responding. Therefore, walking in the Spirit means an individual must be sensitive and in a state of wakefulness and awareness of the Spirit of God.

For an individual to be sensitive to the Spirit of God means that person must have the ability to pick up signals or promptings and respond to them. In our physical world, we have senses to help us navigate our surroundings. Humans have five basic senses: touch, sight, hearing, smell, and taste (known as the big five). The sensing organs associated with each sense send information to the brain to help us process and perceive the world around us. In addition to the traditional big five, there is another sense that deals with how your brain comprehends where your body is in space. This sense is called proprioception. That is the sense of space.

The senses are of no use if there is no consciousness. Here, I'm not referring to any type of consciousness but that which the Lord wants us to always be aware of: Christ consciousness, the consciousness of who you are in Jesus Christ always, and at all times being in remembrance. Consciousness can be defined as:

> The state of being **awake** and **aware** of one's surroundings.

There is a knowledge of God's Word that He wants us to be conscious of once we become believers. Apostle Paul puts it this way.

> Who desires all men to be **saved** and to come to the knowledge of the truth.
> 1 Timothy 2:4

This is what I call the *Priority List (PL)*. The PL is the Lord's desire for humanity in order to establish His Kingdom on Earth as it is in Heaven. I have listed the three-step process below:

1. Salvation
2. Knowledge of the truth
3. Christ consciousness

The most important priority is salvation. It is this work of redemption the word became flesh to accomplish. Whoever accepts this finished work of salvation automatically becomes a new type of creation in existence because of the incorruptible seed (Word) of God. This salvation begins simply by an individual hearing or reading the Word of God, confessing the Lordship of Jesus Christ, and believing in their heart (*see* Romans 10:9).

After salvation comes knowledge of God's Word. A believer without knowledge of God's Word will be subjected to the elements of this world as if they never became "born again." The knowledge of God is the food needed for growth and sustenance for a healthy walk in the Spirit.

The Apostle Peter, recognizing the importance of the Word of God to a believer by the inspiration of the Spirit of God, writes:

As newborn babes, desire the pure milk of the word,
that you may grow thereby
1 Peter 2:2

After an individual accepts the Lordship of Jesus, they're like newborn children. Without the knowledge of God's Word to sustain them, they will be tossed around by doctrines and elements of this world, including society, etc.

Till we all come to the unity of the faith and of the
knowledge of the Son of God, to a perfect man, to the
measure of the stature of the fullness of Christ; [14] *that we*
should no longer be children, tossed to and fro and
carried about with every wind of doctrine, by the trickery
of men, in the cunning craftiness of deceitful plotting
Ephesians 4:13-14

Knowing what His Word says and understanding not only the letter but the Spirit of the Word is the second most important piece of the PL. Whenever an individual comes to a level of understanding and knowledge there is a transformation that occurs.

The proof of knowledge is the liberation it brings.

Knowledge of His word brings about a metamorphosis to our whole being, beginning with our mind. As our mind is renewed with knowledge of His Word, we achieve a state of Christ consciousness, which is the third priority on the PL. In a state of Christ consciousness, the first thing a believer should know is that we are in the Spirit. God is a spirit, and we are born of His Word (Spirit). Therefore, we are of the Spirit of God and in union with Him. We are one spirit with Him (*see* 1 Corinthians 6:17). Let's take a look at this scripture:

> So then, those who are in the flesh cannot please God.
> 9 But you are not in the flesh but in the Spirit, if indeed the Spirit of God dwells in you. Now if anyone does not have the Spirit of Christ, he is not His.
> Romans 8:8-9

This Spirit of God in us is the guarantee for our salvation and proof of our "sonship." Now that we have an understanding of our habitation as believers, let's look at the expectation:

> And those *who are* Christ's have crucified the flesh with its passions and desires. 25 If we **live in the Spirit**, let us also **walk in the Spirit**.
> Galatians 5:24-25

This is so profound, as many believers might not even know that they live in the Spirit, much more walk in the Spirit. The place, habitation, or dwelling every believer should operate from is the Spirit. All inquiries, decisions, and counsel should first take place in the Spirit before the physical. This is important because many are trying very hard to make corrections to the storms in their lives but neglecting to rebuke the wind (spirit) behind the storms.

Let's take an example from the master Himself:

> Then He arose and rebuked the wind, and said to the sea, "Peace, be still!" And the wind ceased and there was a great calm.
> Mark 4:39

When Jesus encountered a storm with His disciples, He first addressed the wind by rebuking it and made a declaration to the sea. He handled the wind, current, and force behind the physical manifestation (boisterous sea) first before talking to the sea. Every believer should learn and understand this spiritual principle. Remember, everything around us is sourced from the unseen Spirit (*see* Hebrews 11:3).

We know the only thing that can defeat darkness is light. Similarly, from the scriptures, we know that the solution to conquering the lust of the flesh is to walk in the Spirit. The way to stop adultery, fornication, uncleanness, lasciviousness, idolatry, witchcraft, hatred, variance, emulations, wrath, strife, seditions, heresies, envying, murders, drunkenness, revelries, and the like is by walking in the Spirit (*see* Galatians 5:19-21).

> I say then: Walk in the Spirit, and you shall not fulfill the lust of the flesh.
> Galatians 5:16

Walking in the Spirit is the antidote for not fulfilling the lust of the flesh. Don't force yourself to try and stop the lust of the flesh. Instead, just practice walking in the Spirit, and that lustful desire of the flesh will be obviated. As we walk in the Spirit, it is the Lord that leads us.

> For as many as are led by the Spirit of God, these are sons of God.
> Romans 8:14

A person is led when they don't know where they're going. The moment you know where you're going, you don't need to be led. What this means for us as believers is that the more we lose our way in Him, the more we find His way in us. Therefore, as sons of God, those yielding to His leading are the matured sons of God.

I would like to introduce some essential senses necessary for walking in the Spirit. Just like our physical senses, the more we exercise them, the more we're able to use them better. Let us look at the following scripture:

And He said, "Go, and tell this people:
'Keep on hearing, but do not understand;
Keep on seeing, but do not perceive.'
Isaiah 6:9

The scripture above indicates two important spiritual senses: understanding and perception. Our spiritual understanding and perception are some of the most vital spiritual senses of a believer.

We hear to understand, we see to perceive.

One day, our Lord Jesus, on addressing the multitude, gave a caution when He said, "…Hear and understand" in Matthew 15:10.

When He had called the multitude to Himself, He said
to them, Hear and understand.
Matthew 15:10

Spiritual understanding is required to understand the things of God. Every believer has spiritual knowledge, which is part of your nature when you become a new being. You were born into Christ with it. However, the spiritual senses need to be exercised for growth. Spirit begets spirit; it takes spiritual senses to detect spiritual phenomena.

Let us look at a story that took place during the early church in Acts of the Apostles, the 14th chapter:

They became aware of it and fled to Lystra and Derbe,
cities of Lycaonia, and to the surrounding region, 7 and
they were preaching the gospel there.
8 And in Lystra a certain man without strength in his
feet was sitting, a cripple from his mother's womb, who
had never walked. 9 This man heard Paul speaking. Paul,

observing him intently and <u>seeing</u> that he had faith to be
healed, ¹⁰ said with a loud voice, "Stand up straight on
your feet!" And he leaped and walked.
Acts 14:6-10

The Greek word *eido* is translated as <u>*seeing*</u> in the scripture
you just read. It also translates: *to perceive, to know, to be aware.*
The Apostle saw with his eyes, but he also perceived faith in
the spirit of the crippled man. This tells us that with our
spiritual perception developed, it is possible to detect or
identify spiritual phenomena such as faith.

In the gospel of Luke, an incident is recorded of Jesus
perceiving the removal of power/virtue from Him. This time,
a different Greek word, *ginosko*, was translated as perceive,
which can also be translated: *to know, to feel.*

Now a woman, having a flow of blood for twelve
years, who had spent all her livelihood on physicians and
could not be healed by any, ⁴⁴ came from behind
and touched the border of His garment. And immediately
her flow of blood stopped.
⁴⁵ And Jesus said, "Who touched Me?"
When all denied it, Peter and those with him said,
"Master, the multitudes throng and press You, [p]and You
say, 'Who touched Me?' "
⁴⁶ But Jesus said, "Somebody touched Me, for I
<u>perceived</u> power going out from Me."
Luke 8:43-46

Our spiritual senses are to be exercised right from the time
we accept the Lordship of Jesus and became new creatures.

For when for the time ye ought to be teachers, ye
have need that one teach you again which be the first
principles of the oracles of God; and are become such as
have need of milk, and not of strong meat.
¹³ For every one that useth milk is unskilful in the word

of righteousness: for he is a babe.
¹⁴ But strong meat belongeth to them that are of full
age, even those who by **reason of use have their**
senses *exercised* to discern both good and evil.
Hebrews 5:12-14 [KJV]

**To discern good and evil means to be awake and
aware in order to walk in the Spirit realm.**

The Word of God put into practice is what exercises and
matures our spiritual senses. The more we use our senses, the
more we can get into the depth of God's Word. However,
when you become a believer, you're introduced to the "milk"
of God's Word.

As newborn babes, desire the pure milk of the word,
that you may grow thereby, ³ if indeed you have tasted
that the Lord is gracious.
1 Peter 2:2-3

The pure milk of the Word is the elementary principles of
Christ (*see* Hebrews 6:1). It is the desire for the Word that
moves a believer from one level of understanding to the other.

But solid food belongs to those who are of full
age, that is, those who by reason of use have their senses
exercised to discern both good and evil.
Hebrews 5:14

But solid food is for full-grown men, for those whose
senses and mental faculties are trained by practice to
discriminate and distinguish between what is morally
good and noble and what is evil and contrary either to
divine or human law.
Hebrews 5:14 [AMPC]

The Amplified version uses two words in the scripture

above that I would like us to examine: the words *trained* and *practice*. We can define training and practice as follows:

Practice: applying what you've learned
Training: learning how to improve something or do something new

Growth is intentional. It starts with a desire, then training by practicing what you have learned in the Word of God. So, how does one train their spiritual senses in order to walk in the Spirit? Below are four simple steps to help a believer walk in the Spirit:

1. Meditate on the Word of God
2. Put the Word first
3. Practice the Word
4. Obey the Spirit of God immediately

Yes, by the time one goes through the first three steps, they would have had their mind renewed to conform with the Word of God, and their conscience washed by His Word. At this level, a believer is capable of picking up prompts from the Spirit of God. This is when a believer studies and understands the communication of the Spirit.

The Spirit of God communicates with us differently and it is critical that you take notice of its uniqueness to you. Never have an expectation based on someone else's experience. You can miss the communication of the Holy Spirit. Every human has a conscience, and believers' conscience has been purged by the blood of Christ as indicated in Hebrews 9:13-14.

For if the blood of bulls and goats and the ashes of a heifer, sprinkling the unclean, sanctifies for the purifying of the flesh, [14] how much more shall the blood of Christ, who through the eternal Spirit offered Himself without spot to God, cleanse your conscience from dead works to serve the living God?

Therefore, it is not unusual at all for the Holy Spirit to speak to us through our conscience. Oftentimes, believers will say: *"something told me to do this"* or *"I didn't feel good making this decision, so I stopped."* All of these are a handful of examples of how the Spirit of God communicates to us. When these communications happen, it is our duty to identify them and respond to them promptly.

CHAPTER 5
Kinetics: Force & Power

Faith is an invisible force. It is a force carrying an enormous amount of power. Force can cause an object to move or maintain a position. Power is the ability or capability to cause a change of state of an object. So, what does force and power have to do with faith?

The physical and spiritual realms are governed by laws, and the laws are sometimes similar in operation. Jesus mentioned one of these laws in the scripture below.

> So Jesus said to them, "Because of your unbelief; for assuredly, I say to you, if you have faith as a mustard seed, you will say to this mountain, 'Move from here to there,' and it will move; and nothing will be impossible for you.
> Matthew 17:20

In the scripture above, we see Jesus talking about the spiritual phenomenon of faith and attributing it to a change in the physical state of an object. Here we see the interaction of two realms. This scripture indicates a tremendous amount of power that can be released by the force of faith as small as a mustard seed.

When you take a look at a mustard seed, as small (1 - 2mm) as it is, it can grow to a height of about 20 feet with a 20-foot spread. In ideal conditions, a mustard tree can get up to 30 feet tall. The mustard seed has all the ability or capability (power) to grow into a vast edifice of a plant if placed in the right environment and conditions. If a physical seed has this ability, how much more a spiritual phenomenon like faith? We know that it is the Spirit that gives life, so the spiritual realm has dominion over the physical.

The magnitude of the power in the force of faith dwells in an understanding of God's Word. You do not have to commit intellectual suicide to believe in the scriptures and have faith. Having faith and growing it does not mean one has to void their intellectual faculties.

I would like to introduce another definition of faith according to the application of the scriptures:

Faith is the response of the spirit of man to the *rhema* in Christ Jesus towards God.

The word *rhema* is a Greek word that can mean a specific personal word spoken by a living thing. In order words, this is the specific word of faith a believer receives from the Holy Spirit in accordance with God's Word.

I'd like to give an example to illustrate what I mean. For instance, if there are two ministers of the Gospel and one ministers at a church in a major city but the other ministers in a city under great persecution of believers. Both ministers were directed by the Holy Spirit to their places of ministry, and both adhered to the Lord's direction. When people see the actions of these ministers, the assumption will be that the one who is ministering in the city under persecution has greater faith than the one ministering in the major city. However, both responded to God's Word. It's easy to be deceived if one looks at the outward actions of people to indicate acts of faith.

And that from childhood you have known the Holy Scriptures, which are able to make you wise for salvation through <u>faith which is in Christ Jesus.</u>
2 Timothy 3:15

Our faith is in Christ Jesus, not the material things one wants to receive by faith. You have faith **in** Christ Jesus that you will receive what you have requested. It is significant where our faith is directed because:

Faith is a vector quantity having both speed and direction.

> Therefore, leaving the discussion of the
> elementary principles of Christ, let us go on to perfection,
> not laying again the foundation of repentance from dead
> works and of <u>faith toward God</u>.
> Hebrews 6:1

The direction of faith is toward God. God is the recipient of our works of faith. That means without faith, it is impossible to please God (*see* Hebrews 11:6).

> For it pleased the Father that in Him all the fullness
> should dwell
> Colossians 1:19

In Jesus Christ dwells all the fullness of God's creation. Therefore, we have unending possibilities when our faith is exercised in Jesus Christ toward God the Father. When faith is aligned and follows the principles of faith operation, it works. Since faith is a response to the Word of God, meaning it requires action, one needs to have an understanding of God's Word.

Let us take an example of this in the scripture. There is a story about a woman who had been bleeding for many years, who finally received her healing when she met the Master: Jesus.

> Now a woman, having a flow of blood for twelve
> years, who had spent all her livelihood on physicians and
> could not be healed by any, [44] came from behind
> and touched the border of His garment. And immediately
> her flow of blood stopped.
> John 8:43-44

I would like to set a backdrop that I think is very important for this incident. The woman the scripture references is someone who, during those times, was not allowed to come among the general population because she was deemed "unclean." Whoever or whatever an unclean person touched became unclean. Therefore, it was a major risk for her to hide herself and sneak into the multitude of people following Jesus.

The scripture is clear that the woman received her healing when she touched the border or hem of the Lord's garment and she became "clean." Why the hem? What is so special about it? Was her action an act of faith?

Jesus Himself confirmed that the woman's actions were of faith and her faith is the reason why she was healed.

> And He said to her, "Daughter, be of good cheer; your faith has made you well. Go in peace."
> John 8:48

Now, let us go back in time before the incident to learn about the hem or border of the garments being worn.

The Hebrew word for hem is *kanaph* and this is the tassels at the four corners of their garments according to the Word of the Lord.

> "Speak to the children of Israel: Tell them to make tassels on the corners of their garments throughout their generations, and to put a blue thread in the tassels of the corners. ³⁹ And you shall have the tassel, that you may look upon it and remember all the commandments of the Lord and do them, and that you may not follow the harlotry to which your own heart and your own eyes are inclined.
> Numbers 15:38-39

Kanaph was a reminder of the commandments of God which is the Word of God. In the scriptures *kanaph* is also translated as wings.

The children of Israel were not strangers to the characteristics of the coming Messiah. This woman who was going through this terrible ordeal knew God's Word concerning the Messiah. The scripture indicated her intention before she took that action of faith by touching the hem of Jesus. She had faith through the knowledge of God's Word concerning the Messiah.

> For she said to herself, "If only I may touch His garment, I shall be made well."
> Matthew 9:21

Now, let us look at the scripture below concerning the Messiah.

> But to you who fear My name
> The Sun of Righteousness shall arise
> With healing in His **wings;**
> And you shall go out
> And grow fat like stall-fed calves.
> Malachi 4:2

The word translated as *"wings"* in the scripture above is from the same Hebrew word, *kanaph*. This means the Son of Righteousness who is in the person of Jesus the Messiah will have healing in His tassel, hem, or borders of his garment.

After suffering for 12 long years going from doctor to doctor and getting no relief, the only thing this woman wanted was her healing. At that moment she took that leap or action of faith armed with the knowledge she had concerning the Messiah. If indeed Jesus was the Messiah, she knew that if she could touch the hem of His garment she would be healed. That knowledge informed her faith, and she acted in Christ Jesus toward God and received her healing.

Whenever principles of God's Word are applied, it works because those principles are supposed to work without any supervision. Whenever principles fail to work, miracles are warranted to correct them.

From the scripture, we see the woman received her healing

without Jesus "supervising" or being aware of the work that power did when it left Him. There were multitudes of people following and touching Jesus yet only one person was able to draw healing from Him. This is remarkable; this is the difference between worshiping God in ignorance versus worshiping Him in revelation birthed out from the knowledge of Him.

> And Jesus said, "Who touched Me?" When all denied it, Peter and those with him said, "Master, the multitudes throng and press You, and You say, 'Who touched Me?' "
> 46 But Jesus said, "Somebody touched Me, for I perceived power going out from Me."
> Luke 8:45-46

Here, we see Jesus using a spiritual sense of perception to determine that power had left Him. That means the power that flows and is activated by the work of faith can be detected.

> Now when the woman saw that she was not hidden, she came trembling; and falling down before Him, she declared to Him in the presence of all the people the reason she had touched Him and how she was healed immediately.
> 48 And He said to her, "Daughter, be of good cheer; your faith has made you well. Go in peace."
> Luke 8:47-48

This is an amazing story, and it demonstrates the ability of the power of God to flow to us and through us. Faith is the conductor that enables the flow of God's power. When the power of God is released, it provides the solution to whatever the need is.

> And His name, through faith in His name, has made this man strong, whom you see and know. Yes, the faith which *comes* through Him has given him this perfect

> *soundness in the presence of you all.*
> Acts 3:16

If the power of God flows through faith, then it is possible for us to hinder the flow of His might. When there is no faith, there is unbelief, and unbelief is a force that negates faith. The scripture narrates an incident where Jesus went to His hometown and could not do many miracles because of their unbelief, which stems from the familiarity of the people toward Jesus as a mere man and not the Messiah.

> *Now He could do no mighty work there, except that He laid His hands on a few sick people and healed them. 6 And He marveled because of their unbelief. Then He went about the villages in a circuit, teaching.*
> Mark 6:5-6

We see another insightful information about faith and unbelief. When Jesus realized the unbelief of the people in His hometown, "*...he went about the villages in a circuit, teaching.*" When there is unbelief, one thing is needed: teaching of the Word. It is through the Word of God that faith is received concerning any situation. For faith comes by hearing the Word of God. Therefore, whatever the situation may be if unbelief sets in, don't sit there quietly. Speak the Word and keep the Word of God in your mouth. As you keep proclaiming God's Word concerning that situation, in no time, the Holy Spirit will take over! *Hallelujah!*

When the Holy Spirit moves, the Word manifests. In the account of creation in Genesis 1:1-3, we see the sequence of events leading to God's Word manifesting.

> *In the beginning God created the heavens and the earth. 2 The earth was without form, and void; and darkness was on the face of the deep. And the Spirit of God was hovering over the face of the waters.*

3 Then God said, "Let there be light"; and there was light.

The scripture above says in part, *"...and the Spirit of God was hovering over the face of the waters. Then God said..."* As a believer, your act of faith is responding to the promptings of the Holy Spirit. In order words, you do not make decisions without the leadership of the Spirit. The power backing our words and actions of faith is a fruit of responding to the Holy Spirit. This is the reason why it's important to develop constant communion with the Holy Spirit. He is a personality and fellowship with Him can save you from a lot of mistakes as a believer. We must remember that the power of God is under the auspices of the Holy Spirit.

But you shall receive power when the Holy Spirit has come upon you; and you shall be witnesses to Me in Jerusalem, and in all Judea and Samaria, and to the end of the earth.
Acts 1:8

The next thing that comes into the life of a believer after the Holy Spirit is the power of God. The power of God is the hallmark of His Kingdom, and every child of God should be introduced to God's power in His Kingdom.

For the kingdom of God is not in word but in power.
1 Corinthians 4:20

Therefore, to know and demonstrate the power of God, we'll need to know who the Holy Spirit is and understand His ministry in the life of a believer. The third person of the Trinity, the Holy Spirit is the one that gives the divine life when a believer is born again. When someone accepts Christ, their "source-life" is supplanted by the life provided by the Holy Spirit, which is a divine life.

The scripture says in 2 Corinthians 5:17:

Therefore if any man be in Christ, he is a new creature: old things are passed away; behold, all things are become new.

The individual is a new creature because the very source of life is new. This individual needs to be studied and understood, just as the body is studied and understood separately from the soul. When an individual is going through any form of psychological issue such as depression, etc., they might go and see a therapist. However, when the same individual gets a burn or a cut on their body, they might go and see a medical doctor. Those two practitioners—a therapist and a medical doctor—attend to different parts of an individual's medical needs. An individual's soul is a byproduct of the reaction between the spirit and the body.

To allow the power of God to be effective in us, we must learn to humble ourselves before the Lord. That is an act of faith. Humbling ourselves before the Lord comprises several things, but I'll highlight just one for our discussion.

Whenever we worry, we do not humble ourselves before Him. So, what should be our response to stress as believers? Let's go through the Word of God, as that is the source of the answer we need.

Likewise you younger people, submit yourselves to your elders. Yes, all of you be submissive to one another, and be clothed with humility, for
"God resists the proud,
But gives grace to the humble."
6 Therefore humble yourselves under the mighty hand of God, that He may exalt you in due time, 7 casting all your care upon Him, for He cares for you.
1 Peter 5:5-7

In the scripture above we see instruction on being submissive to one another, and instruction on humbling ourselves before the Lord. The instruction for humbling ourselves before the Lord is by casting all our cares upon Him.

The sixth and seventh verse says: "…Therefore humble yourselves under the mighty hand of God, that He may exalt you in due time, _casting all your care upon Him_, for He cares for you."

From this scripture, it's clear that casting or laying our cares upon Him demonstrates humility. In that act, we're saying, *"Lord, take control, for we cannot do it on our own."*

God has designed the body, soul, and spirit to respond in certain situations. For instance, when a person gets a cut on their body, the healing process starts right away. The body responds, from the formation of scabs to tissue growth for repair. Similarly, when a person begins to worry, there is a response from the soul. Just like a cut to the body, worrying is a negative phenomenon that affects the soulish man. In order to humble the soul, we fast as believers.

> But as for me, when they were sick,
> My clothing was sackcloth;
> I humbled myself with fasting;
> And my prayer would return to my own heart.
> Psalms 35:13

In other translations, like the King James Version of the Bible, the word *"soul"* is used instead of *"self."* Fasting humbles your soul before the Lord. This is also the natural response to worrying. When one worries about anything or any situation, they begin to lose the appetite for food over time. This is the response of your soul fighting the "worrying state" by causing you to "fast" and therefore humble yourself before God. However, if a believer does not know this truth, they will not be able to act on knowledge to experience the relief they seek.

To sum it up, don't wait for your soul to put you to fast. When you start getting worried about anything, do the following:

1. Start a fast.
2. Cast your cares and worries upon the Lord by praying and letting your request be made known unto Him.

The exercise described above takes practice over time for one to be fully in control of worry by utilizing the power within oneself through faith in the Word of God. I consider worrying to be a negative meditation. There is a difference between thinking to arrive at a solution and worrying. As believers, we think because our Father thinks, and His thoughts are greater. God thinks about us, and He planned and ordained our very paths to success.

For I know the thoughts that I think toward you, says the Lord, thoughts of peace and not of evil, to give you a future and a hope.
Jeremiah 29:11

O Lord, how great are Your works!
Your thoughts are very deep.
Psalm 92:5

I love the last scripture above. It simply implies that great works are products of very deep thoughts. We can look at the universe, galaxies, even our planets and all the ecosystems and their complexities. Indeed, these great works are from very deep thoughts.

CHAPTER 6
Two Forces: Faith & Money

In Chapter 3, we understood that there are two forces as we read in the scripture below. These forces are faith in God and mammon (money).

"No one can serve two masters; for either he will hate the one and love the other, or else he will be loyal to the one and despise the other. You cannot serve God and mammon."
Matthew 6:24

Faith and money are two forces that operate in different realms. That means these two forces have laws that govern them in their respective environments. Below is a list of some of the laws governing these two forces.

Table 1

Faith	Money
A measure/seed of faith is needed to grow your faith.	Seed money is needed in order to increase in wealth.
Without faith, it is impossible to please God.	Without money, it is impossible to please men.
Faith is a legal tender in the spirit realm.	Money is a legal tender in the physical realm.
Faith cannot operate in isolation. Faith is demonstrated by works.	Money is demonstrated by works.
Faith can work with money to produce results in the physical world.	

Before I proceed any further, I would like to bring up a dogma that has been in some Christian faith circles for a while now. That is, *"money is of the devil," "money is evil,"* and the misquoted phrase *"money is the root of all evil."* The scripture is clear on how money can be the root of all evil.

> For the <u>love of money</u> is a root of all kinds of evil, for which some have strayed from the faith in their greediness, and pierced themselves through with many sorrows.
> 1 Timothy 6:10

It is the **love of money** that leads people to pursue all manner of activities, including evil deeds. Money is indispensable in our physical world, the same way our faith is indispensable in the spiritual world. The scripture says:

> But without faith it is impossible to please Him, for he who comes to God must believe that He is, and that He is a rewarder of those who diligently seek Him.
> Hebrews 11:6

We also know that Jesus pleased God, and Jesus is the very source of our faith.

> looking unto Jesus, the author and finisher of our faith, who for the joy that was set before Him endured the cross, despising the shame, and has sat down at the right hand of the throne of God.
> Hebrews 12:2

Every act of faith is rewarded.

From Hebrews 11:6, we see that everyone who believes in God and diligently seeks Him will be rewarded. This is because the action of diligently seeking God is an act of faith. Jesus, being the very source of faith, is rewarded according to scripture.

And being found in appearance as a man, He humbled Himself and became obedient to the point of death, even the death of the cross. ⁹ Therefore God also has highly exalted Him and given Him the name which is above every name, ¹⁰ that at the name of Jesus every knee should bow, of those in heaven, and of those on earth, and of those under the earth, ¹¹ and that every tongue should confess that Jesus Christ is Lord, to the glory of God the Father.
Philippians 2:8-11

It takes faith to obey. The actions we take based on our faith in God's Word place us in a position to be rewarded of God. I would like to talk about just three acts of faith every believer should know and practice:

1. Prayer
2. Fasting
3. Almsgiving

Prayer

Prayer is more than just communication; it's approaching God's grace and mercy. We are told in scripture to come boldly to His throne of grace to receive mercy and find grace when we need it (*see* Hebrews 4:16). The act of prayer should always be based on God's Word mixed with faith.

Is anyone among you sick? Let him call for the elders of the church, and let them pray over him, anointing him with oil in the name of the Lord. ¹⁵ And the prayer of faith will save the sick, and the Lord will raise him up. And if he has committed sins, he will be forgiven.
James 5:14-15

Let's take a look at the scripture we'll be using for the rest of the discussion on these three acts of faith. The Gospel according to Matthew records a teaching Jesus gave to His disciples and multitudes on these acts of faith that I call the **three essential pillars of faith**.

> But you, <u>when you pray</u>, go into your room, and when you have shut your door, pray to your Father who is in the secret place; and your Father who sees in secret will reward you openly.
> Matthew 6:6

There is a reward when we pray and do it the right way. The right way is not praying to receive commendation or reward from man. Therefore, whenever we pray, we are rewarded.

Fasting

Fasting humbles your soul and brings you before God. Fasting involves staying away from **food** but feeding on the Word of God. It is unfortunate that men's opinions and the dictates of this world have caused unnecessary confusion even among some well-meaning believers when it comes to abstinence from food during fasting. The scripture is clear, fasting is <u>abstinence from food.</u> Let's look at how Jesus fasted.

> And when He had <u>fasted</u> forty days and forty nights, afterward He was <u>hungry</u>.
> Matthew 4:2

Jesus was fasting so He was hungry, and He was hungry because He did not eat food. This is so simple to understand. When we stay away from food and focus on the food of the Spirit (scriptures), we set up our soul to be humble before God and receive from Him. Let's look at the following scriptures on how fasting and humbling the soul are related.

Then I proclaimed a fast there at the river of Ahava, that we might <u>humble ourselves</u> before our God, to seek from Him the right way for us and our little ones and all our possessions.
Ezra 8:21

But as for me, when they were sick,
My clothing was sackcloth;
I <u>humbled myself</u> with fasting;
And my prayer would return to my own heart.
Psalms 35:13

When we fast, the scripture indicates that we get rewarded.

But you, <u>when you fast</u>, anoint your head and wash your face, [18] so that you do not appear to men to be fasting, but to your Father who is in the secret place; and your Father who sees in secret will reward you openly.
Matthew 6:17-18

Prayer and fasting are two of the three essential pillars of faith often done together. Each of these three essential pillars is also part of God's greater list of provisions that He has given for our growth in Him. Next, we'll discuss the last pillar of faith.

Almsgiving

Let's start by indicating what almsgiving isn't and charitable deeds aren't. Almsgiving is not: offering, tithing, firstfruit, or general giving to the body of Christ unless the funds are specifically designated for almsgiving. So, what is almsgiving?

Almsgiving is a charitable deed. Hence, giving alms involves providing to a person or group of people in need. This need can be in the form of money or material. In our modern society, there are numerous charitable organizations, and some are very focused on the people they assist. It is quite unfortunate that this is the pillar of faith whereby it seems foreign to believers. Many believers know about their responsibility to fast and pray. However, many are not aware of almsgiving. When the Lord was teaching in Matthew 6, He mentioned these three pillars together, indicating their importance:

> "Take heed that you do not do your charitable deeds before men, to be seen by them. Otherwise you have no reward from your Father in heaven. [2] Therefore, when you do a charitable deed, do not sound a trumpet before you as the hypocrites do in the synagogues and in the streets, that they may have glory from men. Assuredly, I say to you, they have their reward. [3] But when you do a charitable deed, do not let your left hand know what your right hand is doing, [4] that your charitable deed may be in secret; and your Father who sees in secret will Himself reward you openly.
> Matthew 6:1-4

Prayer is as important as fasting, and fasting is as important as almsgiving. The Lord indicated in the verse above that there is also a reward for this act of faith. This is really refreshing, doing a charitable deed is an act of faith according to God's Word.

The scripture tells us a story about a Roman Centurion by the name of Cornelius. The scripture indicated two of the pillars of faith Cornelius was consistent in performing.

> There was a certain man in Caesarea called Cornelius, a centurion of what was called the Italian Regiment, [2] a devout man and one who feared God with all his household, who gave alms generously to the people, and prayed to God always.
> Acts 10:1-2

I would encourage you to read the entirety of Chapter 10 and what transpired with Cornelius as I wouldn't be able to go through the entire story in this book. However, I would like to draw your attention to an interaction that happened between Cornelius and an angel that was sent to him.

The Bible is emphatic that the angelic visitation Cornelius experienced is a result of the actions he had been performing in reverence of God.

> And when he observed him, he was afraid, and said, "What is it, lord?"
> So he said to him, "Your prayers and your alms have come up for a memorial before God. 5 Now send men to Joppa, and send for Simon whose surname is Peter. 6 He is lodging with Simon, a tanner, whose house is by the sea. He will tell you what you must do." 7 And when the angel who spoke to him had departed, Cornelius called two of his household servants and a devout soldier from among those who waited on him continually.
> Acts 10:4-7

It was Cornelius' prayers and almsgiving that caused God to send an angel to him. In truth, the angel said those things became a memorial before God. *This is amazing!* We are seeing what Jesus thought in practice. Now, the question is: How many believers give to charity as much as they pray?

I have been blessed and privileged to be exposed to the Charismatic and Prophetic ministries in my growth in Christ. I remember a testimony a gentleman gave about an ailment that had been plaguing him for many years. During a service, the preacher called the gentleman and mentioned details of the ailment disturbing him. The preacher then proceeded to tell the gentleman that he should look for an orphanage and make a donation, and the ailment would depart from him. The gentleman obeyed and did exactly as he was told, and he received his healing. This is one of the many testimonies concerning almsgiving.

Prayer, fasting, and almsgiving are all part of the provisions the Lord has given to us in our faith walk. As we grow in Christ, we learn when to pray and fast, when to pray and give alms, when to give alms, or when to just pray. Therefore, as believers mature in their faith, the Spirit of God enlightens their understanding of when to use these combinations of provisions from God. All of God's provisions collectively are enough for a believer to mature in the fullness of Christ.

Seed money, just like a seed of faith, needs to be planted for growth. From the scriptures, we know every believer has been given a measure of faith.

> For I say, through the grace given to me, to everyone who is among you, not to think of himself more highly than he ought to think, but to think soberly, as God has dealt to each one a measure of faith.
> Romans 12:3

This measure of faith we have received from the Father needs to be planted for growth, and this is what we'll discuss in the next chapter.

CHAPTER 7
Growing Faith

*"The seed of faith received from the Father is dependent on the
knowledge of His Word."*
Dr. Abankwa

In order to learn how to grow our faith, we need to know
how we receive faith. Earlier on, we established that every
believer has a measure of faith when they're born-again. This
is established in God's Word so that we know we have a
measure of faith (*see* Romans 12:3).

Now, if every believer has a measure or seed of faith, we
have to know how to grow it because seeds are planted. We
are an earthen vessel, and the Lord has planted that seed of
faith in us. For faith to develop, it must be worked out after we
receive it. Faith comes to us through God's Word.

So then faith comes by hearing, and hearing by the
word of God.
Romans 10:17

If faith comes by hearing, then after we hear the Word, what
does the perfection of "hearing" looks like? Another way to
ask this question is: What is the perfection of the hearing
process which will result in faith?

And He said, "Go, and tell this people:
'Keep on hearing, but do not understand;
Keep on seeing, but do not perceive.'
Isaiah 6:9

The process of hearing comes to fruition when we

understand.

We hear to understand, we see to perceive.

So, why is growing your faith important to a believer? It might surprise you to know that when you do a thorough study of the Gospels and search for individual cases of healing, you will realize there are more individual cases of healing recorded where Jesus indicated that their healing was caused by their faith. Below are some example scriptures:

> Then Jesus said to him, "Go your way; your faith has made you well." And immediately he received his sight and followed Jesus on the road.
> Mark 10:52

> Then Jesus said to her, "O woman, your faith is great; it shall be done for you as you wish." And her daughter was healed at once.
> Matthew 15:28

> Then He touched their eyes, saying, "It shall be done to you according to your faith."
> Matthew 9:29

> And He said to him, "Stand up and go; your faith has made you well."
> Luke 17:19

> And He said to her, "Daughter, your faith has made you well; go in peace."
> Luke 8:48

When an individual's faith matures or becomes strong, there are amazing things they can accomplish. The opposite is also true: if an individual is unbelieving or doesn't have strong faith, it hinders their Christian experience. Therefore, it's important for believers to know how to grow the faith they've received. It is that very reason why I am communicating these cardinal truths to you in this book.

I would like to share three fundamental pillars of growing your faith. There is a lot that can be discussed concerning this topic. However, for the scope of this book, we'll discuss the following:

   I.   Receiving the Word
  II.   Meditating on the Word & speaking the Word
 III.   Acting on the Word

   I.   <u>Receive the Word</u>

We have already understood through scripture that one of the ways we receive faith is by hearing the Word of God (*see* Romans 10:17). We also understood that when we hear the Word of God the purpose is for us to understand God's Word. When we gain understanding of the Kingdom message we've received, it takes abode in our hearts. The reception of God's Word is engrafted with faith and it's able to build you up. The believer is built up by faith but must be received.

The Word of God in you is Christ being formed in you. When you become born again, you're born of the Word in Christ Jesus. Now, you are in Him. However, when the light of God's Word starts to make an abode in you, Christ (the Word) forms in you.

Abide in Me, and I in you. As the branch cannot bear fruit of itself, unless it abides in the vine, neither can you, unless you abide in Me.
John 15:4

Now, let's look at what Paul said to the Galatians:

*My little children, for whom I labor in birth again until
Christ is formed in you.*
Galatians 4:19

Thus, the formation of Christ in us is to get to the measure of
Christ to His fullness. To get to this point of growth, the Lord
has placed offices within His body to assist the believer.

*And He Himself gave some to be apostles, some
prophets, some evangelists, and some pastors and
teachers, 12 for the equipping of the saints for the work of
ministry, for the edifying of the body of Christ, 13 till we all
come to the unity of the faith and of the knowledge of
the Son of God, to a perfect man, to the measure of the
stature of the fullness of Christ*
Ephesians 4:11-13

The spiritual growth of a believer is intentional. Just like any
kind of physical growth, you must be intentional about your
diet, nutrients, exercise, etc. Therefore, believers have a focus
on growth, which is the measure of the stature of the fullness
of Christ.

Each office within the body of Christ is needed for the
fullness of the spiritual growth of the body of Christ. The
ministers of God occupying those offices have been given
specific "light" in that office to contribute to the Body to
benefit all. This distribution of light is done through love, and
it is through love that the entire body grows and nourishes
itself. God, in His infinite wisdom, has parted the offices and
gifts of the Spirit; hence, <u>no single minister of God has it all.</u>

If any minister of the gospel begins to think they have all
that is needed for the perfection of the body of Christ, then
they are deceived.

For a believer to grow their faith, the Word of God received must be planted in their heart, with a clean conscience void of offense. The individual also needs an understanding of the Word received to retain it. The Word of God cannot be understood without the ministry of the Holy Spirit. The Spirit of God enlightens our understanding so we're able to comprehend the spiritual realities in God's Word. Scripture interprets scripture, and no word of prophecy or scripture is for individual interpretation.

II.   Meditate on the Word & speaking the Word

Once a believer has received God's Word, what is the next step? We know God's Word is food for our spirit.

As newborn babes, desire the pure milk of the word, that you may grow thereby, 3 if indeed you have tasted that the Lord is gracious.
1 Peter 2:2-3

And I will give you shepherds according to My heart, who will feed you with knowledge and understanding.
Jeremiah 3:15

The Word of God brings knowledge and understanding. When we receive the truths of God's Word, we are to meditate on it. Meditation is a spiritual activity and has specific things that it accomplishes. It's a tool in the spiritual realm. Just like any other tool in the physical, it will work whether you're a Christian or not. Tools are no respecter of persons if you know how to use them to accomplish a purpose. The spiritual activity of meditation is one that hasn't been given enough room for studies in the body of Christ, but it's one of the most vital activities in the growth of a believer. I would need an entire book to delve into meditation as it pertains to believers.

So, what is meditation in the Kingdom of God? After a careful reading of the scriptures and years of guidance by the

Holy Spirit, below is the inspired definition of meditation:

Meditating *on the Word of God is the practice of focusing the mind on the written Word of God – thought or utterance – to train attention and awareness of the soul and achieve a renewal of the mind to align with the Holy Spirit.*

Meditation is like a "silent whistle," or Galton's whistle, that opens the door to your soul, attracting the things of God or the devil. As I indicated earlier on, meditation is a tool that works in the Kingdom of God as well as the kingdom of darkness, just as prayer, sacrifice, and worship.

What meditation does to the soul is like what water does to a planted seed. Throughout scripture, we see the use of the word *"heart,"* which is not the physical heart in your body but the center of your being. This represents who you truly are as an individual. Your mind creates the blueprint, and your heart transforms those blueprints into manifestation. The heart is a storage revealing the real you.

"This is the end of the account. As for me, Daniel, my thoughts greatly troubled me, and my countenance changed; but I kept the matter in my heart."
Daniel 7:28

Then He went down with them and came to Nazareth, and was subject to them, but His mother kept all these things in her heart.
Luke 2:51

Another characteristic of the heart defined by scripture is that it is an incubator producing fruits based on the seeds sown.

> When anyone hears the word of the kingdom, and does not understand it, then the wicked one comes and snatches away what was sown in his heart. This is he who received seed by the wayside.
> Matthew 13:19

The Word of God we receive is a seed that, when well-planted and meditated upon, produces an overflowing bounty harvest. However, if what is sown in the heart is evil, it produces an evil harvest.

> So Jesus said, "Are you also still without understanding? 17 Do you not yet understand that whatever enters the mouth goes into the stomach and is eliminated? 18 But those things which proceed out of the mouth come from the heart, and they defile a man. 19 For out of the heart proceed evil thoughts, murders, adulteries, fornications, thefts, false witness, blasphemies. 20 These are the things which defile a man, but to eat with unwashed hands does not defile a man."
> Matthew 15:16-20

Meditating on God's Word grounds the seed of the Word received into our hearts. This enables alignment with our spirit. Throughout the scripture, we see the patriarchs and men like Abraham, Joshua, and David, just to mention a few, who practiced meditating on God's Word. These men made exploits in their world and provided an example for us to follow.

Our words defile us, in the same manner they can bless us, for what comes from our mouth proceeds from our hearts (*see* Matthew 15:18).

Meditation allows us to make God's Word one with our spirit so we can boldly declare it. We need to proclaim and speak what is written in the scripture concerning us.

Let your conduct be without
covetousness; be content with such things as you have.
For He Himself has said, "I will never leave you nor forsake
you." [6] So we may boldly say:
"The Lord is my helper;
I will not fear.
What can man do to me?"
Hebrews 13:5-6

The alignment of our heart and our confession/speaking is essential in our faith growth. This is the same principle for salvation.

That if you <u>confess with your mouth</u> the Lord Jesus
and <u>believe in your heart</u> that God has raised Him from
the dead, you will be saved.
Romans 10:9

When we meditate on God's Word, belief rises from our hearts and we speak that belief, which grows our faith. As meditation causes God's Word to be grounded in our hearts, the Word eventually comes out of our mouths in our confessions and speech.

A good man out of the good treasure of his heart
brings forth good; and an evil man out of the evil treasure
of his heart brings forth evil. For out of the abundance of
the heart his mouth speaks.
Luke 6:45

God responds to the meditations of our hearts as well as the words of our mouths. There cannot be any effective communication or prayer without the alignment of the heart and the words spoken. A heartfelt prayer is a *meditated* prayer.

Now to Him who is able to do exceedingly
abundantly above all that we <u>ask or think</u>, according to
the power that works in us, [21] to Him be glory in the
church by Christ Jesus to all generations, forever and
ever. Amen.
Ephesians 3:20

A heartfelt prayer is an effective prayer.

These people draw near to Me with their mouth,
And honor Me with their lips,
But their heart is far from Me.
Matthew 15:8

A heartfelt prayer begins from the heart and comes out of the mouth. Sometimes, the prayer doesn't even have to be uttered because the heart is the place of decision-making.

I would like to take you through the story of one such experience. According to scripture, there came a time when Abraham was searching for a wife for his son Isaac. Therefore, Abraham sent his servant to his relatives in Mesopotamia to find a wife for Isaac. Below, we see the prayer of Abraham's servant to God:

Then he said, "O Lord God of my master Abraham,
please give me success this day, and show kindness to my
master Abraham.
[13] Behold, here I stand by the well of water, and the
daughters of the men of the city are coming out to draw
water.
[14] Now let it be that the young woman to whom I say,
'Please let down your pitcher that I may drink,' and she
says, 'Drink, and I will also give your camels a drink'—let
her be the one You have appointed for Your servant
Isaac. And by this I will know that You have shown

74

kindness to my master."
Genesis 24:12-14

Believers are familiar with opening their mouths and praying, as that's what they've been taught. However, there is a heartfelt prayer we see demonstrated throughout scripture.

When Abraham's servant met Laban, he began to elaborate on his mission and experiences throughout the journey. The servant also begins elaborating to Laban about the prayer he said when he was standing by the well. Now, I would like us to read what Abraham's servant said to Laban as he elaborated on his experience, especially in the last verse:

"And this day I came to the well and said, 'O Lord God of my master Abraham, if You will now prosper the way in which I go,
43 behold, I stand by the well of water; and it shall come to pass that when the virgin comes out to draw water, and I say to her, "Please give me a little water from your pitcher to drink,"
44 and she says to me, "Drink, and I will draw for your camels also,"—let her be the woman whom the Lord has appointed for my master's son.'
45 "But before I had finished speaking in my heart, there was Rebekah, coming out with her pitcher on her shoulder; and she went down to the well and drew water. And I said to her, 'Please let me drink.'
Genesis 24:42-45

This is remarkable! The servant's prayer that we read in Genesis 24:12-14 was not spoken by the mouth but by the heart. Everything the servant said in the form of a prayer request to God was said in his heart. This goes to indicate the importance of the heart and what meditation does to the heart in the process of growing our faith.

75

I wanted to touch on prayer because faith is needed for prayer, and a prayer of faith manifests the love of Christ (*see* James 5:13). God does not only answer prayers of the mouth but also prayers of the heart.

Now that we've established the importance of meditating and speaking the Word, we will go into the last part of growing our faith, which is acting on the Word.

III.   <u>Acting on the Word</u>

The Word of God is life, and life is active. The difference between life and death in a body is the activity of that body. Life received from God's Word enables us to be involved in living and acting in accordance with the eternal life we've received in Christ Jesus. In growing our faith, we respond to God's Word by acting on it. We act on His word by praying, fasting, giving, worshiping, etc. For faith to have its perfect way in us–that is, to grow into maturity–we must act on God's Word to produce works of faith.

> What does it profit, my brethren, if someone says he has faith but does not have works? Can faith save him?
> James 2:14

Faith is demonstrated, and the evidence of faith is the works that follow. We are not saved nor justified by works, but we show our works as evidence of faith already at work in us by God's Word. Abraham demonstrated faith by his willingness to sacrifice his son Isaac (*see* Genesis 15:6, Romans 4:3, James 2:23). The Apostle James summarizes this *acting* on God's Word as evidence of faith in one sentence.

> For as the body without the spirit is dead, so faith without works is dead also.
> James 2:26

The spirit of faith is the work of faith we demonstrate as we listen, meditate, speak, and act on the Word of God. Therefore, for our faith to have life and grow, we need to respond to the Word of God by doing what the scripture says concerning us as His children. The Word of God is the Spirit of God, and it's the same Spirit that enables us to conform to the image of Christ.

> But we all, with unveiled face, beholding as in a mirror the glory of the Lord, are being transformed into the same image from glory to glory, just as by the Spirit of the Lord.
> 2 Corinthians 3:18

As we look into the Word of truth, there is a transformation that is supposed to happen. That transformation will occur when we act on the Word. It is quite unfortunate that some have been looking into this same Word of truth but haven't been transformed because they fail to act on the scriptures.

> Therefore lay aside all filthiness and overflow of wickedness, and receive with meekness the implanted word, which is able to save your souls.
> 22 But be doers of the word, and not hearers only, deceiving yourselves. 23 For if anyone is a hearer of the word and not a doer, he is like a man observing his natural face in a mirror; 24 for he observes himself, goes away, and immediately forgets what kind of man he was. 25 But he who looks into the perfect law of liberty and continues in it, and is not a forgetful hearer but a doer of the work, this one will be blessed in what he does.
> James 1:21-25

When we do the Word, we produce the works. You cannot

be a doer of the works without knowing His Word. All the patriarchs of faith produced works of faith. This is the testimony concerning Abraham:

> He staggered not at the promise of God through unbelief; but was strong in faith, _giving glory to God_;
> 21 And being fully persuaded that, what he had promised, he was able also to perform.
> 22 And therefore it was imputed to him for righteousness.
> Romans 4:20-22

Can you give glory to God when what He has said concerning you hasn't happened yet? Can you give glory to God when what you're going through in your life is not consistent with His Word given to you?

It takes strong faith to give glory to God when you haven't seen what was promised, but you have the evidence in your spirit. It takes strong faith not to stagger, and it takes strong faith not to be double-minded. Therefore, in order to grow a strong faith and have the "faith of God" (_see_ Mark 11:22), we need to practice:

1. Receiving the Word
2. Meditating on the Word & speaking the Word; and
3. Acting on the Word.

As you train your spirit by practicing these activities, may the God of hope help you grow your faith in Him, and may all the glory be onto His name. Amen.

ABOUT THE AUTHOR

Dr. Kevin Abankwa is passionate about the knowledge of God's Word. He loved the Lord from a young age, and his knowledge of God's Word has only grown over the years. In this book, "*The Enigma of Faith,*" he shares some of the insights the Spirit of God gives him as he studies the Word of God. Dr. Abankwa is a chemical engineer, data & analytics scholar, and entrepreneur. He earned his doctoral degree in business administration – data analytics at Grand Canyon University. He lives in North Carolina, USA, with his wife and three children.

[f] [o] @kevintheauthor

Email: kevintheauthor2020@gmail.com

Milton Keynes UK
Ingram Content Group UK Ltd.
UKHW020647201123
432908UK00019B/2465